THE POWER OF EVE

It's Not What You Think

GIGI BLACKSHEAR

Rain Publishing

KNIGHTDALE, NORTH CAROLINA

Copyright © 2014 by **Gigi Blackshear**

All rights reserved. No part of this publication may be reproduced, distributed or transmitted in any form or by any means, including photocopying, recording, or other electronic or mechanical methods, without the prior written permission of the publisher, except in the case of brief quotations embodied in critical reviews and certain other noncommercial uses permitted by copyright law. For permission requests, write to the publisher, addressed "Attention: Permissions Coordinator," at the address below.

GiGi Blackshear/Rain Publishing
PO Box 702
Knightdale, NC 27545
www.rainpublishing.com

The front cover features the art and design of artist Henry Lee Battle: http://HenryLeeBattle.com

Editing: www.RainPublishing.com

All scripture quotations and references are from the New King James Bible translation and are public domain in the United States.

Ordering Information:
Quantity sales. Special discounts are available on quantity purchases by corporations, associations, and others. For details, contact the "Special Sales Department" at the address above.

The Power of Eve/ Gigi Blackshear. -- 1st ed.
ISBN 978-0-9908453-3-1

Library of Congress Control Number: 2014953867

The Power of Eve is dedicated to all those who encouraged me by thought, word or deed! Your words and actions propelled me forward when I wanted to quit! Your care and concern held up my arms when they got tired! God is the giver of gifts and talents! Thank you for helping me make good use of mine!

CONTENTS

The View From the Dust 1
   Questions for Thought and Discussion: 4
In the Beginning 5
   Questions for Thought and Discussion: 9
The Power of the Union 11
   Questions for Thought and Discussion: 14
Adam Speaks 15
   Questions for Thought and Discussion: 18
Pride and Haughtiness 19
   Questions for Thought and Discussion: 22
The Power of Persuasion 23
   Questions for Thought and Discussion: 25
The Path of Least Resistance 27
Life Outside the Garden 31
   Questions for Thought and Discussion: 34
Power: It's not what You Think 35
   Questions for Thought and Discussion: 39
The Spirit of Jezebel 41
   Questions for Thought and Discussion: 44
Repentance 45

Questions for Thought and Discussion:	48
Restored to New Life	49
Questions for Thought and Discussion:	51
Walking in Faith	53
Questions for Thought and Discussion:	56
Growing in Grace	57
Questions for Thought and Discussion:	61
Reclaiming the Power	63
Questions for Thought and Discussion:	66
Fit For Battle: New Life in Christ	67
Questions for Thought and Discussion:	70
Epilogue	71

> *Now the serpent was more cunning than any beast of the field, which the Lord God had made. And he said to the woman, "Has God indeed said, you shall not eat of every tree of the garden?"*   *Genesis 3:1*
>
> *And the Lord caused a deep sleep to fall on Adam, and he slept; and He took one of his ribs and closed up the flesh in its place. Then the rib, which the Lord God had taken from man, He made into a woman, and He brought her to the man.*   *Genesis 3:21-22*

Prologue

As I walked through the doors of the sanctuary, I felt like what I imagined the woman with the issue of blood felt. I was in so much pain that even though I walked upright, in my spirit I was bowed over. In my mind's eye, everyone could see how broken and damaged I was. As I made my way to the front, I instinctively felt that this was where I belonged. I did not know it at the time, but God had led me to the place where I would receive my greatest blessing. He led me to the place where I would finally recognize and understand the power that He had placed within me, the power of Eve.

CHAPTER ONE

The View From the Dust

"What is this man, made in the image and likeness of God? Was I not here before him? After all, am I not the most cunning beast of the field? Why then, was I not given charge over the garden? Now, must I too be brought to him, to be named? What shall this one with so much favor call me? I know that I was created for greatness, created to rule! Therefore, I will wait. The day is coming when my name will be great! Moreover, when that day comes, when the opportunity presents itself, I will be ready."

Ever the observant one, the serpent takes notice of the woman, her delicate beauty and her lovely voice. More importantly, he notices the effect she has on Adam. How he longingly looks at her when she is not watching, how he instinctively gravitates towards her anytime she is near.

He studies the way Adam touches her skin and smells her hair and senses the way she enters his thoughts as he goes about his day. The serpent instinctively knows that there is power in the way they joyously come together and become one. "There is something more here, it is in her and I must find it! I must study her; I must discover her power for it is what makes him weak," the serpent declares.

The serpent knew that there was power in the union, in the relationship between the man and the woman. He also knew that they were both oblivious to the power that together, they possessed. Because he recognized the woman's power, he also recognized the power of the union. He understood that together they would be an impenetrable force! So he devised his plan, a plan to divide and conquer!

Later, in the cool of the evening, the serpent finds Eve admiring the flowers of the garden. He recognizes this moment as his opportunity and speaks to her with beguiling charm rolling off of his forked tongue, "Is not this the most beautiful garden you have ever seen?" he asks Eve. "Serpent", Eve replies, "This is the ONLY garden I have ever seen." "Then I must be right!" he declares. "How wonderful it must be to partake of all of the fruits in the garden and that nothing is off limits to you." "You are wrong serpent," says

Eve, "there is one tree that we cannot eat of, the one in the midst of the garden. God has said if we eat of the tree of knowledge of good and evil we will surely die!" The serpent lies to Eve, telling her, "You will not surely die! For God knows that when you eat of the tree, you will be like the most high!" As Eve looks longingly at the fruit, the serpent knows that he has won.

Did you notice the serpent's arrogance? How he beat his own chest, how he attempted to exalt himself, even over God's greatest creation? It is this arrogance that will be his downfall. Isn't it sad to see one with great intelligence and potential make the fatal mistakes that come with arrogance and pride?

The bible says, "Pride goes before destruction and a haughty spirit before a fall." We know that the serpent did indeed fall, and those spirits, pride and haughtiness, continue to cause falls and destruction even today.

Questions for Thought and Discussion:

1. In the story, the serpent studied Eve. Do you think your actions and behaviors are being studied today, and if so, by whom?

2. What, if anything, could Eve have done differently?

3. What can you do to prepare yourself to handle spiritual and/or moral confrontations?

CHAPTER TWO

In the Beginning

The first thing recorded in the bible, after God created woman and brought her to Adam, was that she was paid a little visit. I have often pondered why the serpent visited the woman and did not pose his question to Adam. Scripture tells us that he was more cunning than any beast of the field. Growing up in the church, I heard many sermons on the subject, most of them preached from a male perspective, leaning toward the woman being considered the "weaker" sex. For some reason, I had not been able to buy into that particular train of thought. It seemed to me that, because he was so cunning, perhaps the serpent recognized something about the woman that even she, herself, did not recognize. The serpent recognized the power that the woman possessed.

The bible tells us that the woman, after being enticed by the serpent, took of the fruit, did eat, and gave to her husband and he did eat. How is it that even though Almighty God had given Adam instruction not to touch the tree and not to eat of the fruit, was the woman able to get Adam to eat? Perhaps it was her feminine wiles, her ability to convince, that powerful force we all possess. In order to be Adam's help, Eve had to have enough power to get him to listen to her. I believe if the woman had been conscious of the power that she possessed, we would still be in the garden, living lives of ease. Imagine, just for a moment, that the woman had used her power to rebuke the serpent, how very different our lives might be today.

Had she only recognized the tactics that were being used against her, she would have been able to warn her husband, after all, she had been created to be his help. But instead of using her power to rebuke the serpent, she used her power to persuade her husband. She even used the words of the serpent, "we will not surely die" to convince her husband to eat of the forbidden fruit.

As it is with sin, I imagine that the pleasure of eating the forbidden fruit was short lived. The bible records that as soon as Adam and Eve had eaten the fruit that their eyes were opened and they knew that they were naked. Adam and Eve hid themselves between the trees and we have been hiding ever since.

When God discovered what Adam and Eve had done, he spoke first to the serpent, cursing him to spend all of his days on his belly, eating of the dust. God put enmity between him and the woman and between his seed and her seed. Women, now we know why we take off running when we see a snake to find a man to come and kill it! Interestingly enough, God cursed the serpent, but He did not curse Eve. He only punished her. Eve's punishment was five-fold. To the woman, God said, "I will greatly multiply your sorrow and your conception, in pain you shall bring forth children, your desire shall be for your husband, (and, here's the big one), he shall have rule over you!" Up until that point, Eve was God's beautiful creation. After that, Adam became her ruler.

Because of Adam's disobedience, God cursed the ground from whence Adam had come and made him toil for the rest of his life in order to survive. Could this be why it is so very hard to get our men to listen to us? Think about our interaction with men today. It usually takes quite a bit of work to get them to actually listen to what we have to say and even if we can get them to listen, it is even harder to get them to take our advice. It is hard to believe that something which took place so long ago would still affect our lives today, but we know that our actions have far reaching consequences.

As for the serpent, the curse of being made to spend all of his days upon his belly pretty much dashed his grand plan for greatness and domination. We don't really know the nature of the relationship between the serpent and man before Adam's disobedience, but we know that fear was not a part of it because he spoke freely with Eve in the garden. After that, because God put enmity, or deep hatred between the serpent and the woman, between his seed and her seed, he would have been pretty much forced to steer clear of human contact. In his arrogance, the serpent's actions condemned him to a life of isolation and a lifetime fearing retribution.

Questions for Thought and Discussion:

1. *Eve convinced her husband to eat of the forbidden fruit. Have you ever convinced or dare I say, enticed someone to do something they should not have done? Were there negative consequences to your actions?*

2. *Once their eyes were opened and they knew they were naked, Adam and Eve hid themselves from God. Have there been instances in your life that you wanted to hide from God? Rather than hide, what would be a better alternative?*

3. *From the story, it appears that there was a lack of communication between Adam and Eve. Do you have difficulty communicating with the male figures in your life? How can what you've read here help you in this area?*

CHAPTER THREE

The Power of the Union

Isn't it interesting that the serpent recognized the power of the union between Adam and Eve? I imagine that he had to have witnessed a coming together of the other species in the garden. Was there something special about Adam and Eve coming together? The bible records that after God created Eve and brought her to the man he said, "This is now bone of my bones and flesh of my flesh, she shall be called Woman, because she was taken out of man." The bible says, "…therefore shall a man leave his mother and father and shall cleave unto his wife and they shall be one flesh." And therein lays the power of the union!

One flesh. The man and the woman. I believe that because the woman was taken out of man, when they are apart, he is always lacking that which is missing. However, when they become one flesh in the strength of the union, the man's original power is renewed. When cleaving to the woman, the way God designed, man is his most powerful, most complete self. No wonder the serpent wanted to bring division in the union. It is my belief that God never intended for Adam and Eve to live and act independently of each other. They were created as two parts of one whole. Long before Eve, Genesis 1:27 says, "So God created man in his own image, in the image of God created he him, male and female created he them."

God's plan was that together, the man and the woman would forever have dominion over the earth. We know now that the serpent had another plan, a plan that would bring division and separation between man and his God and between man and his woman. The division that was created that fateful day in the garden has spanned generations and is still an issue in relationships today!

Along with division, something else was introduced in the Garden that day, deceit! The serpent lies to Eve and for the first time dishonesty is seen in the garden. Interestingly enough, if he actually believed what he told Eve, he would have just eaten the fruit himself. Instead he lied and deceived poor Eve. Being alone in the Garden may have caused her to be vulnerable to the attack of the enemy. Scripture says, "Our adversary, the devil goes about as a roaring lion, seeking whom he may devour." In the garden this day, he found Eve.

Does that mean that as women we are never to be alone? I don't believe that to be true. However, as women, I believe that God created us to always have a covering. I believe God intended that we would grow up and mature under the care of loving parents. The man would leave his mother and father to find a wife, which he would take from the care of her parents into his care. The two would then become one flesh (again) and would live happily ever after. So much for fairy tales, for in most cases, that is not what we have or where we find ourselves today.

Was the power of the union destroyed that fateful day in the garden? No, I believe that it is still very much attainable. But I also believe that in order to experience it, the Adams and Eves of today must have an understanding of their original purpose, individually and corporately. They were created to have fellowship with God and to have dominion on the earth.

Questions for Thought and Discussion:

> 1. Why do you think the serpent recognized the power of the union between Adam and Eve and they did not?
>
> 2. Adam called Eve "bone of my bone and flesh of my flesh." How does that speak to your role as a woman?
>
> 3. Do you agree that there is strength in the union between a man and a woman?
>
> 4. If yes, what is the purpose of that strength?

CHAPTER FOUR

Adam Speaks

The first words Adam spoke in response to God's questioning in the garden were, "That woman you gave me, she gave to me the fruit and I did eat." Not only did he throw Eve under the bus, he actually attempted to implicate God! Notice Adam says, "That woman you gave me," as if the problem was in God's decision to give him a woman.

I imagine God, looking at Adam and shaking his head, thinking to himself, "This boy is as dumb as a box of rocks, perhaps we should just scrap this one and start over." However, being the loving and forgiving God that we know Him to be, he only punished Adam. Willful disobedience and the punishment he received took Adam away from his beloved garden and created the first recorded division between man and his God.

The biblical account does not tell us of Adam's thought process during this time. What must he have felt, knowing that he had disappointed his father, knowing that his disobedience had changed the nature of his relationship with God? Prior to this act of defiance, Adam had no secrets from God, no need to hide anything and no need to fear. This one act had far reaching consequences, for it not only changed the course of Adam's day-to-day existence, it also changed the way God viewed Adam. Because God is omniscient and had himself created man with free will, He was not surprised by Adam's actions. I imagine that, as a parent with a wayward child, God was saddened that Adam chose to be disobedient.

Was Adam's disobedience willful? Did he rise up in defiance and declare, "Never mind what God has said, I will do as I please?" I don't believe his disobedience to be willful, but more of taking the path of least resistance. Adam probably had every intention to obey God. What may have happened to Adam is possibly what happens to each of us when faced with the choice to walk in obedience or disobey, to stand firm or succumb to peer pressure. Sometimes we crumble. Imagine this, beautiful, naked Eve, standing there holding the fruit out to Adam, smiling and saying, "You know you want some!" Tell me what man could resist that? We know the rest; Adam succumbed to his fleshly desires and paid dearly for his sinful disobedience, as it is with all humans. Sometimes we allow our flesh to dictate our actions and we end up doing things that we know are wrong, even things that we don't want to do! The bible tells us the wages of sin is death and instead of living in the garden forever, man was destined to work out his days toiling the earth to eventually die. We don't hear much from Adam after this account. Obviously, he obeyed God in that he was fruitful and multiplied! And so we are here.

Questions for Thought and Discussion:

1. *Adam and Eve knowingly disobeyed God. Have you ever knowingly disobeyed God? If so, how did you feel afterwards?*

2. *Where can you find help when faced with the choice to walk in obedience or disobey?*

3. *After choosing to disobey God is there anything that you can do to make things right again?*

CHAPTER FIVE

Pride and Haughtiness

One definition of pride is an excessively high opinion of oneself. I suppose the serpent, who himself wanted to be like the most high God, foolishly thought rather highly of himself. So high in fact, that he enticed God's creation in an attempt to gain dominion. Many a mortal man has allowed himself to become lifted up in pride to his own hurt. Prideful thinking has caused the downfall of many sisters as well. Looking at my own life, I can recall times when rather than seek out help; I would suffer in silence because I was too prideful to let anyone know that I had a need. Because things looked pretty good from the outside, it was easy to hide the real truth.

I believe that the problem with pride has more to do with the fact that when we think so highly of ourselves that we feel we are above being helped, we rob others of the opportunity to be a blessing in our lives. Now when you couple pride with conceit or arrogance, you have a recipe for disaster. And so it was with the serpent.

If, as the bible says, pride goes before destruction and a haughty spirit before a fall, then we are all in trouble. Haughtiness can be a calling card for some sisters. It is one thing to be prideful, but haughtiness takes it to another level. The spirit of haughtiness causes us to look down our noses at others, as if we are somehow responsible for our own successes. The problem with this is that it does not take into consideration that all that we are and all that we have is by the grace of God and in most cases, has very little to do with us.

I imagine that for the serpent, it was a personal affront to be subject to Adam. After all, God had called him forth first. Perhaps he felt that it was his "birthright" that he should have been given dominion over the earth. Whatever the reason, his haughty spirit did indeed lead to a fall, not only his, but Adam and Eve's as well, as we know from the story.

Being prideful, in and of itself, may not be an unpardonable sin, actually, it probably does more damage to the one filled with pride than to anyone else. However, the effects of haughtiness can be seen and felt by others, therefore, I believe, making it even more insidious. Pride and haughtiness first showed up in the garden, unfortunately it did not stay there.

Questions for Thought and Discussion:

1. Has the spirit of pride ever shown up in your life and what were the effects of it?

2. While it may not be a bad thing to be proud of your own or someone else's accomplishments, how much pride is too much?

3. Do you know someone who is haughty? How do you feel about that person and why?

4. Is there such a thing as Godly pride? How does this show up?

CHAPTER SIX

The Power of Persuasion

The serpent used it on Eve and she used it on Adam. What new skill was this that had been so effectively used to wreak havoc in the garden? The ability to persuade or convince was displayed masterfully by the serpent. He used words in such a way that made what he was saying seem harmless, even though they were in direct conflict with what God had said. Was it just his mastery of words or were there other actions that went along with the words to make his attack successful?

When we communicate with one another it usually involves more than just words. Our bodies have a language of their own. Think about your most recent interaction, did you motion with your hands, did you smile or laugh? All of this is communication and I believe that when you are trying to persuade or convince someone of something, all of this is magnified, especially in interactions between the opposite sexes. Women, you know, a well-placed touch has been known to work wonders in helping us have our way.

In the animal kingdom, some types of animals are said to have the ability to charm their prey and perhaps this was what took place in the garden. Perhaps Eve was charmed into disobedience. I am not surprised because many of us have been charmed into doing things that were not in our own best interest. Is it possible that Eve learned this skill from the serpent? After all it had worked so well on her, why wouldn't it work on Adam? Unfortunately, it did work on Adam, so well in fact that it caused him to sin.

The power of persuasion is not necessarily a bad thing. In all honesty, when used to accomplish something positive, it can be a very good thing. But as with anything, there will always be room for abuse and those who will abuse. I believe that what took place in the garden, if not abuse, then at a very minimum, was a misuse of this power and we are all still reeling from the effects of it.

Questions for Thought and Discussion:

> **1.** Do you think it is a good thing to use persuasion in dealing with others?
>
> **2.** Have you ever used persuasion to get something you wanted? How did you feel afterwards, powerful or sorrowful?
>
> **3.** Do you believe using persuasion is morally or ethically wrong?
>
> **4.** How do you think God views persuasion?

CHAPTER SEVEN

The Path of Least Resistance

In the Garden of Eden, Adam and Eve lived a life of ease. There were no worries and no difficulties. Their only responsibility was to dress and keep the garden. God had already provided everything they needed to live happily ever after. His only instruction was that they were not to touch the tree of the knowledge of good and evil, which would seem to be an easy thing to do considering that they had many other trees from which to eat. I have often wondered what dynamic was in place, perhaps in Eve's mind or in Adam's thought process during this time that made eating the fruit the thing to do. Was it just easier to agree with the serpent, take the path of least resistance and just go along, or was there something else?

Taking the path of least resistance, or choosing to do the things that are the easiest, have been a pitfall for many. In the beginning of the story, Eve did offer some resistance to the suggestion of the serpent, but she didn't resist very long. Under pressure from the serpent, Eve folded! Perhaps if she had held to her argument long enough, Adam could possibly have come to her rescue. But, rather than holding her ground, Eve went along right down the path that led to destruction.

The interesting thing about resistance is that by its very definition it is designed to build strength. I imagine that our Omniscient God was standing by observing the entire scene being played out in the garden, all the while hoping that his children would not take the path of least resistance, but that they would stand strong in obedience. Perhaps He allowed them to be tempted by the serpent because He wanted them to develop strength and character. Perhaps He knew that living a life of ease without obstacles or resistance would not be in their best interest. Perhaps He allowed the temptation to develop trust and faith, things they would need later in their walk with Him and with each other.

Even though it appeared that she was, Eve was not alone in the garden. When faced with the choice to take either the path of least resistance or a seemingly more difficult path, it is helpful to know that whatever the choice, you are not walking alone. I believe that when presented with the choice, all Eve had to do was call out to God, who is a very present help in the time of trouble. If nothing else, this one action might have struck fear in the heart of the serpent, causing him to flee. Taking the path of least resistance may seem the easiest path to take, however in the long run, it is usually the most costly. Instead of taking the path of least resistance, how about resisting the devil? James 4:7 says, "Submit yourselves to God, resist the devil and he will flee from you."

CHAPTER EIGHT

Life Outside the Garden

I imagine what life must have been like for the happy couple after God banished them from the garden. So much for marital bliss! I see Adam, leaving his beautiful garden and life of ease to toil a cursed ground. Moreover, what of the woman? Sorrow, conception, pain, and desire for one who had been given rule over her. Can you imagine a life without sorrow or childbirth without pain? What about being ruled by a man who blames you for his act of disobedience?

The biblical text does not say that Adam was angry, but who wouldn't be? The dynamics had changed. Now instead of being "bone of my bone and flesh of my flesh," the gift of God became "the woman who got me kicked out of the garden." Let us not forget about the serpent. Adam probably went on a snake hunting expedition that was out of this world!

So Adam worked the earth with the sweat of his brow and Eve, in pain, bore children. What a contrast, life before disobedience and then life after banishment. I'm pretty sure this explains the dynamics that play out every day right here, right now.

The world continued on, as I imagine, did the war between the sexes, the one that began with God giving Adam rule over Eve. After being condemned to toil the ground, the bible says that Adam named the woman Eve, which being translated, means mother of all living. The next thing we see is God making clothes for Adam and Eve. I'm also pretty sure that part of Eve's punishment was to have to wear a bra, that part just came later.

Let's imagine that Adam and Eve somehow managed to adapt to life outside of the garden and settled into the rigorous routine of making a living and building a life. Even though the work was hard, it stands to reason that they were able to find some patches of happiness in their union. After all, Eve was probably still a very beautiful woman and being the resourceful woman that God created to be a help to the man, surely she was wise enough to get back into the good graces of her husband. The first thing she probably did was give him sons, to help him toil the earth. I imagine that she lived out her days looking to God, raising her children, and being subject to her husband.

The bible tells us that Eve bore Adam sons, Cain and Abel, one a shepherd and one a husbandman. Cain murdered Abel which caused him to be banished by God to roam the earth. As a mother, I can only imagine the pain and grief Eve must have experienced at the death of one son and the banishment of the other. Perhaps, this too was part of her punishment, to watch the effects of her sin pass from one generation to another. We do not hear a lot about Eve, the mother of all living, from here on, but we know her story continues.

Questions for Thought and Discussion:

1. God placed Adam and Eve in a beautiful garden. Is there anything that God has created that would remind you of what the Garden must have been like?

2. According to the story, Eve probably got back into the good graces of her husband by giving him sons. Would that work today?

3. What have you done to restore peace back into your home after an argument or disagreement?

CHAPTER NINE

Power: It's not what You Think

The serpent tried to capture it, Adam was intoxicated by it and Eve misused it! What was the source of this great force that changed the course of humankind? Had God intentionally created Eve with something within that would drive her away from himself? No. The rib that was used to create her was one of the strongest bones in the body, for it protected the fragile heart. Therefore, Eve undoubtedly had been given the physical strength necessary to be a help to her husband, but that was not her power. I believe that when God took the rib from Adam, He used it to create Eve in such a way that neither would be complete without the other. I also believe that His intention for their union was that they would act as one.

Had Eve first consulted her husband prior to partaking of the apple, there might have been a very different outcome in the Garden.

For so many of us today, it is important that the make-up is flawless and the hair is fierce. The manicure is tight and the pedicure is perfect. Smelling like Armani and wearing Michael Kors, we stand in front of the mirror and ask, "Do I look good enough? Will he like what he sees?" These are the questions the flesh asks, because it seeks the approval of man. The reason we put so much energy and effort into the outside appearance is because we have been foolishly led to believe that this is where our value lies. The problem with physical beauty is that it fades. If that is where you have placed your value or from where you gain your self-worth then you have done yourself a terrible disservice.

It is true; God did indeed grace Eve with beauty, natural beauty. This was definitely not something she could have attained from outside of herself. Eve was beautiful on the outside because she was beautiful on the inside, as are you, daughter of Eve, beautiful inside and out. Yes, God gave Eve physical beauty, but in order that Adam would have a daily reminder of the artistry of his father. The same One who painted the heavens and sprinkled it with stars, created Eve, and that is the same One who created you. He painted you ivory and bronze, sculpted your curves and mounds. A marvelous masterpiece, He made you, woman! But, that is not the power.

The helpless woman routine that we see on display every day, you know, the batting of the eyelashes and the sashaying of the hips, the salacious licking of the lips and even the eyes welling up with tears at just the opportune moment is not the power either. While all of these things may appear effective, they are at best, a feeble attempt to counterfeit the power, at worst manipulation. And we know the effects of manipulation.

We have been led to believe that power is the same as control. The ability to control others may give us a sense of power; however exercising control over someone else speaks less about us and more about the person allowing themselves to be controlled. Very rarely do you see the truly powerful usurping the control of others. They understand that true power is about giving and in giving you receive.

Looking back at the garden, God gave Adam and Eve authority over everything. He also gave them free will, or the ability to choose. He could easily have blocked access to the tree or silenced the serpent, but He did not. If an all-powerful God did not use His power to control Adam and Eve, why would we want to use power to control others? Having the ability to manipulate and control does not make us stronger, it actually makes us weaker and more vulnerable. The power of Eve is also not control.

Questions for Thought and Discussion:

1. *Have you ever used manipulation to cause things to go your way?*

2. *What was the outcome? Has anyone ever manipulated you to do what they wanted you to do? How did that make you feel?*

3. *What does your "helpless woman" routine look like? How effective is it and do you consider this to be manipulation?*

CHAPTER TEN

The Spirit of Jezebel

Remember the biblical account of Jezebel, who used manipulation to persuade her husband to worship pagan gods? She was said to have persecuted the prophets of God and to falsely accuse Naboth, a wealthy landowner, of blasphemy, causing him to be put to death. The Bible says that she consequently met a terrible death. Thrown out of a window by members of her own court, her corpse was eaten by stray dogs. Scripture records that prior to meeting her demise, Jezebel "painted her face and tiered her head" (put on make-up and a wig or adornments in her hair) and looked out a window. Sound familiar?

Jezebel was a woman of beauty and intelligence, but what she was lacking was spiritual wisdom. She encouraged her husband to stop serving God and turned his heart to the worship of idols. Once again we see a woman in the role of a manipulator. I believe this spirit of Jezebel has been passed down through generations. Often we see beautiful, intelligent women, sacrificing themselves at altars of false gods such as lust and deception. Using sex and illicit relationships to mask feelings of loneliness or unworthiness, we at times, have given our bodies at the risk of losing our very souls and in this day and age our lives.

Today, many women have college degrees but less wisdom, more success but less self-worth, more substance but much less satisfaction. Reality is, in trying to find themselves, some have become more lost than ever. Looking outside ourselves to find completeness in others, we have neglected to seek the one who has been calling us back to himself ever since the garden.

Think about the women you know, the beautiful, intelligent ones that have made one poor decision after another. How about the ones wasting away in bad relationships with men who are clearly not worthy of the gifts being offered to them? Using every available resource, these women give and give. When giving fails, they take and put up with whatever is dished out. After being rejected, some have even gone as far as to cause physical harm to the objects of their desire or even sadder, to themselves. Perhaps it is the spirit of Jezebel that has them bound to the belief that they can somehow get these men to love them in return. Ironically, because men are hunters by nature, they usually don't value what takes no effort on their part to acquire.

The outcome of manipulation is hardly ever positive. It is rooted in selfishness and runs contrary to the nature of God. We have been led to believe that Jezebel was a whore and nothing more, but Jezebel was a woman, just like you and I. She was a woman who wanted what she wanted and was determined to have it at any cost.

Daughters of Eve, if this spirit of Jezebel has shown up in your life, take heart! There is hope and help in the arms of a loving father and He has made a way for you to be delivered and restored.

Questions for Thought and Discussion:

> 1. Based on what we know of her, what do you think was Jezebel's greatest sin?
>
> 2. What would you take away from the story of Jezebel's life?
>
> 3. Jezebel died a horrible death. Do you think it was justified? Why or why not?

CHAPTER ELEVEN

Repentance

Here is where I imagine Eve's story picks up, left alone while Adam worked the fields. Eve had plenty of time to ponder the life she set in motion by allowing herself to be beguiled by the serpent. Although she was able to go about the tasks at hand, her mind and thoughts must have often took her back to that fateful day in the garden. I wonder if she berated herself for being weak and vowed to never allow herself to be used in such a way again? I'm sure her heart ached because of the separation she felt from God, and she likely sought redemption through prayer. I believe she poured out her heart to God and begged forgiveness, for herself and for her husband. God heard her prayers and honored her petition and all is well again because a broken spirit and a contrite heart He would not despise. Although they could never return to the garden, God gave grace and mercy to one He loved so dearly and restored Eve.

Here, daughters of Eve, is where we come in. How many of us have followed Eve's example, allowing ourselves to be beguiled and then used to our own hurt? How many of us have gone down the wrong road, made poor choices or just plain messed up? I would venture to say that we have all, at some point or another, been Eve. We have also, at times, used our beauty and our bodies to do the beguiling and yes, once again, to our own hurt. Perhaps also like Eve, we vowed, "never again will I allow myself to be used and abused." As daughters of Eve, along with her beauty, we also inherited her sinful nature and thus fall victim repeatedly to the adverse effects of sin. Because the bible does not specifically tell us that Eve repented of her sin, I have only speculated here, but considering that the "apple", pardon the pun, does not fall far from the tree, we would do well to follow other examples in scripture of seeking and receiving forgiveness. The same way Jesus forgave the woman who was about to be stoned for committing adultery (John 8:1-11), and offered the Samaritan woman at the well living water (John 4:1-26), He has made a way for you. You see, like Eve, you are still God's woman, His beautiful creation and He loves you.

Daughters of Eve, have you come to that place of recognition? Have you yet realized that the only hope for you lies in the forgiving bosom of a loving God? Has God led you to the place where you can receive deliverance and healing? There is no coincidence in God; the fact that you are holding this book in your hands means that God has met you right where you are and He is waiting for you to repent and be restored.

The act of repentance simply means to review one's actions, confess your wrong doings to God and commit to make the necessary changes, or better yet, make a change of heart, mind and actions. Perhaps the notion of repentance is foreign to you, if so, do not be dismayed. It is merely stopping right where you are, turning from wrong behavior and acknowledging that you have done wrong and asking forgiveness from a patient, long-suffering and loving father. Once you have done this, in the same way that I believe He did with Eve, God will hear and restore you to your rightful place in him.

Throughout the bible we find stories of repentance and restoration. God is constantly seeking to restore fellowship with His beloved children and anxiously waits for us to come back to him. Remember, God went to the Garden seeking fellowship with Adam and Eve and He desires fellowship with you.

Questions for Thought and Discussion:

1. *Have you ever had to ask for forgiveness for something that you did? How did that make you feel afterwards?*

2. *Are there things in your life right now that you are sorry for and feel you need to be forgiven? Have you asked for forgiveness? If not, why?*

3. *Repenting not only means being sorry, but also committing to changing your behavior. Do you have a heart of repentance for wrongdoing?*

4. *Have you repented of your sins and accepted Jesus Christ as Lord and Savior of your life?*

CHAPTER TWELVE

Restored to New Life

To restore something means to bring it back to existence, or to its natural state. How wonderful it is to know that God can bring a dead life back to existence, back to the original state in which He created it. Restoration gives us a clean slate, another opportunity to live the life He had originally planned and purposed for us. Wouldn't you welcome an opportunity to begin again?

What does a restored life look like? I imagine, to God, it looks like the sky after a terrible thunderstorm. There are no remnants of the storm in the sky. It looks as if there has never been a storm, ever. The sun is shining, the birds are singing and there is a rainbow. Because God is the one doing the restoring, it is as if the transgressions never took place. There is no memory bank in heaven that holds transgressions. The bible says He throws our sins into the sea of forgetfulness never to be remembered again. Isn't that good news?

Now that you have been restored, what is the next step? Even though God holds no records of our transgressions, we still possess our memory. In order to successfully maneuver our new lives, we must renew our minds. Remember earlier I said repentance was a change of heart, mind and actions? Well, our minds need to be regenerated and this can only be done by spending quality time in God's word. Eve had one up on us in that she had direct access to the Father. Ephesians 4:23 tells us to be "renewed in the spirit of your mind and put on the new man which after God is created in righteousness and true holiness" (KJV).

Renewing your mind is not a difficult task. It does, however, take commitment on your part. A commitment to take time daily to pray, read and study God's word. Our Father still seeks to meet with you in the garden, in the quietness of the morning when there are few other distractions. Daughter of Eve, when you do this, you open up yourself to all that God wants to impart to you. Remember, it is the word of God that renews. Your responsibility is to take it in and let the word do its work.

Questions for Thought and Discussion:

1. *God is a restorer. Are there areas in your life that need restoring?*

2. *Restoration is only part of a transformed life. Renewing of the mind takes work on your part. Are you willing to do the work to have a renewed mind?*

3. *Making a commitment to spend time in prayer and study of God's word is a sacrifice. You may need to let go of other things in order to make time for the things of God. What are some things you can let go of to make time for God?*

CHAPER THIRTEEN

Walking in Faith

In times past, we walked according to our fleshly desires. We lived our lives doing what felt good and what we thought was right, sometimes. Other times, we did what we knew was wrong. We entered into relationships with the wrong men, for the wrong reasons because we were walking in darkness. You know what happens when you stumble around in the dark? You stub your toe, that big one that gets in the way, or worse, you fall down.

The good news is that God, in His infinite wisdom, allows us to survive the stumps and stumbles. According to Romans 8:28, "we know that in all things God works for the good of those who love him, who have been called according to his purpose." We can take comfort knowing that even the stumps and stumbles will ultimately work together for our good.

Now that we have exercised our faith and received grace, how do we walk out these new lives that we have so been blessed to receive? Once we have accepted the precious gift of salvation and forgiveness of our sins we become new "creatures." The bible says, "Behold, all things are made new," but what of our flesh? How do we navigate our new lives in Christ, yet still live in sinful, fleshly bodies? It all begins with the renewing of the mind. Philippians 2:5 says "Let this mind be in you, which was also in Christ Jesus." Having the mind of Christ entails thinking differently and behaving differently. Christ made himself of no reputation and took on the form of a servant. Therefore, it matters not, who you were, only who you are right now. Having the mind of Christ means humbling yourself, because Christ, though He was fully God, humbled himself even unto death on the cross.

Scripture records that because He humbled Himself, God highly exalted Jesus, giving him a name above every name. He wants to do the same for you, daughter of Eve. Jesus walked in obedience to the will of His Father. Therefore, so should we. For in walking out our lives in obedience, we are working out our own soul salvation.

In the life of every Christian, there will be times of temptation, testing and trial. Working out your own salvation does not mean having the ability to save yourself. It means that in times of temptation, you draw strength from the word of God. By spending time in prayer and study of God's word, you grow stronger in order to resist temptation. It is in obedience to the word of God that we discover the will of God. And it is in the will of God that you will find peace.

Questions for Thought and Discussion:

1. *In times past we walked according to our flesh. Now that you are living a life of faith, what is one thing you can do to help you in your Christian walk?*

2. *In walking out our own salvation, there will be times of testing and trials. This is where fellowship with other believers becomes vital. What can you do to become connected with other Christians?*

3. *Being taught the word of God is a key element in spiritual maturity. There are many different denominations and church fellowships. Have you connected with a ministry that is preaching and teaching the word of God?*

CHAPTER FOURTEEN

Growing in Grace

Growing is the process of becoming larger and more mature through natural development. The bible speaks a lot about growing and even more about maturing. Take the analogy of a seed; in order to grow into a plant or a tree, it must first go into the ground. That means being covered by dirt. Then it must suffer a death of sorts. In order to be transformed, it must first die to its seedling nature. So it is with us, in order to mature and grow, we must first die to our sinful nature. In the same way that the seed receives nourishment from the soil, in order to grow in grace we must receive nourishment from the word of God. 1 Peter 2:2 says "As newborn babes, desire the sincere milk of the word that ye may grow thereby". Growth is a process that requires diligence and patience. Our responsibility as new creatures in

Christ is to remain diligently committed to becoming more like Christ.

By now, some of you are asking, "Do I really have to be covered in dirt?" Or, "What if I'm lactose intolerant? I don't know about this "milk" thing." Rest assured God knows you. In fact, because He created you, He knows all about you. He knows you will fall, fail and fall again. That is why you are not made of glass and why He made provision for your restoration. Remember, He is an all seeing and all-knowing father and He loves you.

Think back over your life, to the times when you were covered in "dirt" or better yet, doing "dirt." Think about the circumstances and situations that you thought were going to be the death of you. In retrospect, now that you have survived, come through, and been delivered, those things don't seem so bad after all. Do they? Have you ever wondered what purpose a particular hurt or trial served? I discovered something about the scripture that says "all things work together for good." Some of my most painful "things" were actually working together for the good of someone else, someone who God was going to bring into my life, someone who needed to know that they too could survive that particular hurt.

It may be difficult to understand that a loving God would use your pain to help someone else, but think about the biblical stories. They are all there to serve as examples for us. Keep in mind, God does not cause our calamity. However, because we recognize that He is in control, we know that whatever befalls us has been sifted through His hand and whatever He allows serves a divine purpose.

Scripture says that God sits as a refiner and purifier of silver. In the process of being refined, the metal must be put into the fire. The silversmith sits directly in front of the fire the entire time the process is taking place. He knows that he must watch to ensure that the metal does not stay in the fire too long, as it would be destroyed. He is there watching in order that he can remove the metal as soon as it is ready. How does he know when to remove the metal from the fire? The refiner knows that the silver is ready to come out of the fire once all of the impurities are burned away. Then and only then can he see his own image in the metal. Are you not more valuable than silver? Of course you are!

Daughter of Eve, take a look in the mirror, past the bad hair day hair and the blemishes. Look beyond the bumps and the imperfections, those first things you see when you look at yourself. Look deep into your own eyes, long enough to see beyond the hurt and the pain. If you look long enough and deep enough you will begin to see what the refiner sees, the beauty that is hidden deep within. The beauty that he knows has been there all along.

Right now you may be in the midst of the fire. You may feel like Shadrach, Meshach and Abednego in the fiery furnace, but know this, you will not be destroyed. You are only being refined. The impurities and imperfections of living a sinful life are being burned away. Keep in mind the refiner is right there with you. His role is not an easy one, for he knows that the fire is hot. He knows that you are crying out for deliverance and although it is painful to watch, he also knows that there is value in trial and tribulation and you will come forth as pure gold, if you keep the faith.

Questions for Thought and Discussion:

1. *The growth process can at times be painful. As we leave behind old habits and addictions. But God is refining you as pure Gold. What are some of the things that you are glad to be free of from your old life?*

2. *There is freedom and liberty in your new life with Christ. What do you enjoy about being a Christian?*

3. *As you mature in the things of God, He will prepare you for service. What gifts and talents do you have that you can commit to the service of the Lord?*

CHAPTER FIFTEEN

Reclaiming the Power

Power - now that you know what it is not, how do you reclaim it? Daughter of Eve, you reclaim the power by recognizing what you are, your true, God given value. You are a diamond! Didn't you know? Look at how you sparkle and shine! You can multi-task because like a diamond, you are multi-faceted. You are like the hardest substance on earth, yet your softness melts hearts. For thousands of years diamonds have been valued for their strength, brilliance and beauty. Created in high-pressure and high temperature conditions, their beauty shines through. Daughters of Eve, is that unlike you? Think of your own high pressured, hot tempered life, yet you continue to sparkle and shine.

In the life of a diamond, how deep it is cut determines how it reflects light and consequently, how much it sparkles! Do you feel that you have been cut to the core by wrong left turns, failed relationships and poor choices? Know this, diamonds don't break when dropped! A diamond's clarity is based on how many flaws are found in it. So perhaps this explains why being dropped reveals clarity! After you have been mistreated, carelessly handled or thrown away, if you are open to it, clarity is revealed.

The word diamond comes from the Greek word αδάμας which means unbreakable. That, along with its clarity and beauty has led it to represent pure, everlasting love and that is the purpose for which you, daughter of Eve, were created! He gave you strength, beauty, and brilliance, but more importantly, because God is love, he created you for love!

Now that you know how truly valuable you are, that you are a diamond, created for love, reclaim your power and walk in it! Deep inside of you is the power to carry and bring forth life. The world needs what you have. Satan tried to exploit it, the world has tried to counterfeit it, but you still embody it and it is the thing that will change the world. Daughter of Eve, your power is love! And that really is all we need. You see, John 3:16 records "for God so loved the world that He gave His only begotten son, that whosoever believes on him should not perish, but have everlasting life".

The key word in John 3:16 is gave. This love is demonstrated by giving. First by giving your life to God, who then enables you to see yourself as He sees you, a chosen vessel, to bring true and everlasting love to a lost and dying world. And in giving of yourself, love grows and expands and encompasses all it touches.

Questions for Thought and Discussion:

1. You are a diamond! God created you beautifully. How can you use your beauty as a reflection of your Heavenly Father?

2. Now that you know your true worth, how will that play out in your everyday life?

3. You are precious to God! How will knowing this change the way you relate to yourself and the way you view others?

CHAPTER SIXTEEN

Fit For Battle: New Life in Christ

Now when you look in the mirror, what do you see? Do you see your beloved self, the one that God gave His son to die for? Of course you do! Because the entrance of the word gives light and light dispels darkness. Once you recognize that you were created for love, you can give love and receive love in the purest sense, the way God intended. There is something different now about the way you walk and the way you talk. Does it feel like there is lightness in your step, almost as if you are being carried? My dear daughter of Eve, it is because you are now being led and guided towards your new life in Christ. There is calmness and a peace that you have never known before and this peace will keep you, not only you, but those you love and care about.

No longer are you seeking after that which has eluded you for so long. You already have everything you need because now you are walking with God. And yes, in His presence is fullness of joy. Your gifts are materializing and your calling is becoming clear. Where there was once misappropriated desire, there is a passion to do the Father's will. There is much to be done and he has blessed the work of your hands. The grace and mercy that has been shown to you, you will gratefully bestow on others.

You thought you were the only one, but look around. There are other daughters and they so desperately need what you and I now have, they just don't know it yet. There is a battle going on! The battle is for the minds, hearts and souls of your sisters. The serpents of this world have not stopped beguiling and deceiving. The same way he attempted to bring division between Adam and Eve in the garden, he is still manipulating and misleading today. He has no new tricks. But you, daughter of Eve, recognize his tactics. Because you have been restored, you can sound the alarm. You can help arm your sisters for battle.

Are you your sister's keeper? I'll let you answer that for yourself, just remember, you were once her and "To whom much is given, much is required." Sharing your new life is such a small price to pay for all that you have received. God himself has equipped you to serve. Yes, the battle is raging, but you, daughter of Eve, are more than a conqueror. The power of Eve is love and love conquers all. God is calling! Will you answer?

Questions for Thought and Discussion:

> 1. Thinking back over your life, what experiences have you survived or been delivered from that you thought you'd never make it out of?
>
> 2. Do you think hearing from other women survivors would have helped you?
>
> 3. Do you know other women, maybe friends or family members struggling with the same issues?
>
> 4. Do you think hearing your story could make a difference?
>
> 5. Are you willing to share your pain in order that someone else might be helped?

Remember, to whom much is given, much is required and you have been equipped for battle!

Epilogue

By now you may be asking yourself, what gives this author the right to tell me how or what I should be? She doesn't know me, or what my life is like! But that is where you are wrong. You see, not only do I know you, I am you. The prologue at the beginning of the story is my story, at least part of it. The reason I shared it is because although, I may not have the right to tell you what to do or how to live your lives, I do have a responsibility. I have a responsibility to care about each and every one of you and a responsibility to share my life and my stories as a sacrificial offering because I know what God saved me from and I now know for what purpose I was saved, to stand on the mountain tops, to go out into the highways and byways to tell of His healing power, deliverance, grace and mercy and to stand by your side in battle. The woman who was bowed over in her spirit is now fit for the fight, standing strong inside and out, her brokenness forever healed. Because of love, God did it all and remember, He is no respecter of persons. What he has done for me, he is waiting to do for you and others like you!

ABOUT THE AUTHOR

Gigi Blackshear, a native of Jacksonville, Florida, is a dedicated member of Spirit of Life Worship Center, where the Pastor is Reverend Mark L. Griffin; Gigi serves as Sunday school teacher and Steward Board member. As a Certified Christian Life Coach and founder of Conscious Choice Coaching, she teaches that we can all create the lives we desire, one choice at a time. Gigi is helping clients of all ages see their true value and worth according to the word of God. Gigi has been writing for many years as a credit union marketer and newsletter editor. A passionate, motivational speaker, Gigi uses her gift as an encourager to help build up the kingdom of God. She published her first book, *Thank You for the Pain: Poems and Reflections on the Journey to Gratitude* in 2011.

The mother of two wonderful adult sons and three beautiful grandchildren, Gigi loves to travel and enjoys spending time with her family and beloved dog, Duncan.

Additional copies of this book can be purchased from Rain Publishing and online bookstores.
www.rainpublishing.com

You can also mail your request to:

Please include the following with your order: Title, number of copies, shipping address, contact information, payment ($9.99 x # of copies) including shipping ($5.00), and mail to:

Gigi Blackshear/Rain Publishing
PO Box 702
Knightdale, NC 27545

www.ingramcontent.com/pod-product-compliance
Lightning Source LLC
Chambersburg PA
CBHW072104290426
44110CB00014B/1821